ABOUT THE BOOK

Everybody—from the smallest child to the great Pelé—is playing soccer! It's easy to learn, the equipment is inexpensive, and above all, it's a great game.

In this exciting book author Howard Liss recounts the history of soccer in the United States, including the rise of the superstars, and introduces young readers to the fundamentals of soccer—the rules of the game, the various plays, and the basic skills. Step-by-step, in photos and text, young soccer buffs will learn the techniques of kicking, heading, trapping, throwing in, goal-keeping, and tackling. Also included is a special section on conditioning—getting in shape to play the game.

Photographer Bruce Curtis focuses his camera on children of all ages playing soccer—from the youngest, who at four and five are just learning to play, to teenagers improving skills in a soccer clinic, to expert amateur league players—boys and girls—who travel all over the world playing matches.

Soccer—the fastest-growing team sport in America—is a game for everyone to enjoy. And *The Great Game of Soccer* is a book that all soccer enthusiasts will delight in reading.

THE GREAT GAME OF SOCCER

by Howard Liss

photographs by Bruce Curtis

G.P. Putnam's Sons · New York

For my nephews,
Murray Gudisman and Harvey Flick.

LIBRARY OF CONGRESS CATALOGING IN PUBLICATION DATA
Liss, Howard
The great game of soccer.
Summary: Traces the evolution of soccer from a rough-and-tumble free-for-all
into the world's most popular spectator sport and outlines the game's rules.
1. Soccer—Juvenile literature.   2. Soccer—History—Juvenile literature.
3. Soccer—Rules—Juvenile literature.   [1. Soccer]   I. Curtis, Bruce.   II. Title.
GV943.25.L57   796.33'42   78-9842   ISBN 0-399-20644-2

Designed by Bobye List

CONTENTS

THE HISTORY OF SOCCER

SOCCER IS ONE OF THE OLDEST TEAM sports known to man. Some historians say that a soccerlike game was played in China about 2500 years ago. The Chinese called the game *tsu chu*. It was played with a ball made of leather, which the teams tried to kick over a silk net that was strung between two 10-foot-high bamboo poles. At that time it was more a military contest than a sport, and the play was very rough, especially when the Emperor was watching. According to some legends, the winners were rewarded with gifts, and the captain of the losing team was flogged.

The Romans also played a game similar to soccer, which they called *harpastum*. They used a ball made of the inflated bladder of an animal, which they kicked or shoved toward some kind of goal.

Most of the early stories about these soccer-like, kicking games indicate that, in one way or another, the sport was begun by the military.

Sportsmanship is very important in soccer. Here, young players from the Hicksville, Long Island, Soccer Club shake hands with members of the opposing team following a match.

The most popular of all stories tells of the Danish invasion of the English town of Kingston (some historians say it was the town of Chester, but that does not really matter) in medieval times. The people of the town fought bravely until help arrived and the Danes were all killed. To celebrate their victory, the townspeople cut off the head of the Danish leader and kicked it around the streets. Afterward, the victory was commemorated on Shrove Tuesday of every year with a kind of "kick-ball" game. But the game resembled a riot. Everybody in the village kicked and shoved and punched each other, trying to get at the ball. If the ball happened to fly into the river, they all went in after it.

As the years passed, the popularity of kicking games continued to grow, but the sport had both advantages and disadvantages. For example, during these "contests" the participants suffered broken bones, bloodied heads, and loosened teeth. On the other hand, history tells us that the games helped cool off a couple of wars. The English and the Scots were engaged in a bitter feud that lasted for many years. But few pitched battles were fought because it was difficult to find good soldiers. The young men of both lands had given up practicing archery because they preferred to face each other on the soccer fields. The skills of battle became so neglected that in 1365, King Edward III of England banned the sport completely. But it was still hard to enforce the law, because it

Game action at Hicksville.

seemed that everybody liked to play or at least watch the mobs of people banging and shoving each other, just because of a ball.

In Scotland, there were women's teams. They called the game "melleys," and the married women played against the unmarried women. Melleys was more a brawl than a game, as the women fought and kicked to gain possession of the ball.

For centuries there were no widely accepted rules for any of the kicking games. A team might consist of a hundred players, or even a whole village. There was no strategy and no organization, and so nobody knew what he or she was doing, and probably nobody cared. Once, a French nobleman watched a match while visiting in England. He shook his head sadly and remarked, "If this is what the English call playing, it would be impossible to describe what they call fighting."

The rules changed all the time, probably to suit the players. When a new rule or two was tried, a different game often resulted. That was how Gaelic football started, sometime in the sixteenth century. No one really knows which new regulations were suggested, but today's Gaelic football can be called a cross between soccer and basketball. Teams consist of 15 players. The ball can be kicked like a soccer ball, or punted like a football, or dribbled like a basketball, or even punched. However, it cannot be carried or thrown.

This young athlete plays amateur soccer on an all-girl team for the Hicksville, Long Island, Americans. She and her team have traveled all over the world to participate in amateur soccer matches.

Rugby was born in the same manner. In 1823, during an intramural game at the Rugby School, a boy named William Webb Ellis suddenly picked up the ball and ran it across the goal line just as the tower bell sounded, ending all activities of the day. At first his teammates were angry because he was breaking the rules, but then they decided it was not such a bad idea to run with the ball after all. Today there is a tablet set in the ground at the school, with the words:

This stone commemorates the exploit of William Webb Ellis, who, with a fine disregard for the rules of football as played in his time, first took the ball in his arms and ran with it, thus originating the distinctive features of the Rugby game.

Probably the incident at Rugby School showed that soccer had to have a standard set of rules. Many teams were competing against each other by then, including Eton, Rugby, Harrow, Winchester, Cambridge, Oxford, and others. But, before every game the team captains had to meet and decide on the rules. Sometimes they could not agree at all. For example, Rugby School insisted that it was all right to carry the ball, but other schools did not want that rule in the game. Finally, those in favor of ball-carrying split off to form their own Rugby Union.

Progress in establishing standard rules was made, but it was slow. It was not until 1890 that referees were given the power to call a foul; before that, players were expected to observe the rules on the "honor system."

Soccer was so popular at the time, that a kind of professional soccer was being played. The rules for the pro games were even less established.

Actually, the players were "semipros." A team hired a player and then found an easy job for him with an employer who was an ardent soccer fan. If the worker did not show up for work on time, but was away practicing or playing, that was perfectly all right. That was really why he was hired in the first place.

But that system did not work very well. All too often a team would steal another team's star player with the offer of a better job, and there was nothing anyone could do to stop it. With few standard rules, things were in a state of confusion. Sometimes a team would fail to show up for a match, or, when the teams did play, one was often so much better than the other that the game was a joke. Once a team called Preston North End slaughtered another team called Hyde United by the score of 26–0!

In 1888 a Scotsman named William McGregor established rules for a true professional league. Schedules would be planned, and the teams *had to* play. Players had to stick with a team. They would no longer work at a job arranged by a local fan who happened to own a factory. They would be paid to play soccer. A scoring system was devised to rank the teams: each team received two points for a victory, one point for a tied game, and no points for a loss.

The new league started with 12 teams, but soon many more teams were added, so that the league had to be divided into *divisions*. The best teams were in Division I, the next best in Division II, and so on. At the end of a season, the two lowest ranked teams of Division I were demoted, or relegated, to Division II, while the two top ranked teams of Division II were promoted to take their places. Both the scoring system and the demotion–promotion rules are followed in today's British soccer leagues.

Undoubtedly, the British did more to promote soccer throughout the world than any other nation. England once had a magnificent navy, and colonies all over the globe. British soldiers and sailors took their favorite pastime with them, wherever they went, and the game's popularity spread. Spain, Portugal, and other countries, which also loved the game, did the same. And yet it took a long time before soccer became popular in the United States. This was due to the stubborn refusal of one influential college, Harvard, to "play by the rules"—and also the invention of several other popular team sports.

2
SOCCER IN THE UNITED STATES

IT WOULD SEEM THAT EVERY YOUNG-ster walking down a road likes to kick at a tin can, or a stone, or some other object. Since soccer is primarily a kicking game, it should have been popular in the United States from the start. What happened to stop the progress of the sport? Why did "soccer-style football" split apart from "American-style football"?

During the early part of the nineteenth century, the students at Princeton, Harvard, and Yale played a soccerlike game using the inflated bladder of a pig. Like their counterparts in Europe, the American players cared very little about rules, and they too played a rough-and-tumble game. At Harvard, especially, the game was very violent. On the first Monday of every school year the lower classes engaged in a "rush," which saw the "players" piling on, punching, and kicking each other, forgetting all about the ball. The day came to be called *Bloody Monday*, and finally the situation got so out of hand that school officials put a stop to it.

An all-out effort. In Hicksville, children play soccer from the age of four or five, and the Hicksville Soccer Club has produced many fine players, both boys and girls, of the best amateur caliber.

After some years, however, the officials relented, and permitted some form of soccer to be played, provided the players used their common sense and stopped trying to maim each other. It remained a game for the brave, but fewer players were sent to the infirmary.

By 1855 a round rubber ball was in use, which enabled players to learn to kick with at least some degree of accuracy. Oddly, boys in junior schools established rules before their older brothers in college did. This was especially true of the junior schools in the Boston area, including the Dixwell School, Boston Latin, and others.

The college students still could not agree on how they wanted to play the game. For example, some schools permitted players to "baby" (dribble) the ball, others did not. Some teams insisted on 25 players to a side, others wanted more or fewer players.

As it happened, both Princeton and Rutgers had many similar rules, and since they were located fairly close to each other, it was suggested that these two rival colleges play against each other. On November 6, 1869, they did compete.

It has become accepted to call this the first intercollegiate football game. In truth, it was no such thing! If anything, it might be called the first intercollegiate *soccer* game, because kicking was still the most important part of the sport. However, the players could catch the ball,

Two players vying for the ball in a college soccer game.

which modern soccer players (except for the goalkeeper) are not permitted to do. But actually, it was neither soccer nor football as we know the games today.

Several other colleges, including Columbia and Yale, decided to play soccer against each other. Harvard was invited to join the group, but they declined. They preferred their own version, which they called "the Boston game," which was somewhat like soccer and somewhat

C. W. Post College teammates congratulate each other after a game well played.

like rugby, yet was not really like either game. For instance, one of Harvard's rules permitted a player "to run with the ball if pursued." No one was quite certain how to interpret that rule, but the players liked it anyway.

Still, Harvard was anxious to compete against another college, and it was learned that McGill University, in Montreal, Canada, played rugby. McGill challenged Harvard and Harvard accepted but most of the rules they agreed to play

by were the ones Harvard players were more familiar with. Wonder of wonders, Harvard won!

The McGill team taught the Harvard men a few basics of their rugby-type game. And Harvard decided to break new ground with their Boston game by challenging Yale. All of *football*, both soccer and American style, was about to undergo a dramatic change. Soon each would go its separate way.

Then came the contest that has come to be known as *The Game*. On November 13, 1875, a match was arranged between Harvard and Yale. It was mainly a rugby match with a few soccer rules added. The players could run with the ball whether "pursued" or not. Tackling was permitted but only above the waist. A touchdown scored no points, but it did give a team the opportunity to kick a field goal, which was worth one point.

Harvard won, 4–0. If any single game can be called the first intercollegiate *football* game in America, that was it, and *not* the Princeton–Rutgers game six years earlier. There was tackling and there was ball carrying, two of the fundamentals of American-style football, neither of which is permitted in today's soccer.

Two Princeton students, W. Erle Hodge and Jotham Potter, watched the first Yale–Harvard contest. Perhaps, watching the two traditional rivals on the field, the men of Princeton recalled the tales of how rough soccer, too, had been half a century earlier. Perhaps they had become bored with soccer because it was too tame and they wanted more physical contact. Whatever the reason, Hodge and Potter helped to change the rules of Princeton's game to conform to those of Harvard and Yale. And it was not long before Columbia was added to the list.

Over the years soccer was always forced to play second fiddle in popularity to another sport. At first it was baseball. When the immortal Cincinnati Reds came upon the scene in 1869 with their unbeatable team, baseball became king. Added to soccer's woes was the popularity of American-style football. Then, in 1891, James Naismith invented basketball, which found instant favor with American fans. And there was also ice hockey to challenge soccer. Perhaps it was because the other sports were American and soccer was European; ice hockey might have been born in Canada, but still, that was part of North America.

Soccer did not die out, but for a long time, all through the first half of the twentieth century, the game had only a few fans. Several colleges had soccer teams, particularly those in the northeastern part of America. There were also some amateur teams, which played for the sheer love of the game, and a scattering of professional leagues across the country. The most highly rated of the professional leagues was the American Soccer League, which included teams such as the New York Giants and the New York

This Hicksville player is determined to beat Syosset.

Game action, Hicksville vs. Syosset.

Listening to a pep talk before the game.

Americans. The Western League included a team from St. Louis, and one called "The Chicago Bricklayers." There were a few ethnic organizations, such as the German–American Soccer League. One of the finest of all soccer clubs was the Hakoah All-Stars, composed only of Jewish players. They played excellent soccer, often defeating visiting championship teams from other nations.

Those were difficult years. Nobody seemed to care about watching or playing soccer, and there was little coverage in the newspapers. Even the *New York Times*, which tried to cover all sports, seldom gave more than one paragraph to soccer, and then only if it was an important game. Since the newspapers did not print many soccer items, the sport had almost no chance to grow, to attract new fans.

As an example, in 1932 the New York Giants played New Bedford for the ASL championship. The match was held at the Polo Grounds, where baseball's mighty New York Giants played their home games. Only 3000 fans turned out to watch the soccer championship game. That same year, the Hakoah All-Stars met and defeated the championship team from Canada. A mere 3500 fans saw the action. But better times were coming, and it was due in part to television.

In the early 1950's, American-style football began to be aired on television. The fans loved to watch games, especially pro football with its rough action. Professional football teams, which had struggled along before, suddenly became rich. Several colleges, which had given up their football activities, began to field teams again.

But not all schools could play American football, for many reasons. Some rural schools had only a few students, ranging in age from 6 through 18. Also, football is an expensive sport, because it requires full uniforms, shoulder pads, strong pants, helmets, and other equipment. Even a high school team must have 25 or 30 players, and equipping all these players costs a great deal of money.

Football is also a complicated game, using tricky plays and formations. There are a great many rules and regulations to learn. A small school cannot always afford to hire a good coach to explain everything. Yet, the older boys in small schools wanted to play an outdoor game during the colder months.

Well, soccer was a kind of "second best" sport, wasn't it? There were very few rules and regulations to learn, and there was no need to buy the costly gear necessary for football. Nor did a player have to be 6 feet tall and weigh 200 pounds. Anyone—boys and girls—could participate as long as he or she possessed agility and stamina. Thus more and more schools began to play varsity soccer.

The Hicksville "tiny tots" in a summertime practice game. Children of four and five learn to play soccer —and love it.

American professional soccer changed when, in 1967, the North American Soccer League was organized. However, soccer did not suddenly take the place of football. In fact, football and pro soccer did not compete at all, since football remained an autumn game and the NASL played during spring and summer. Of course there was competition from baseball, so soccer continued to struggle along.

In sports it has always been true that big crowds can be attracted by big stars. Many years ago, Babe Ruth was the big attraction in baseball; pro football did not have many fans until Harold "Red" Grange began to play. What U.S. soccer needed was a superstar, one the fans would gladly pay to see in action. There was one such player—indeed, he was the greatest soccer player of all time. His name was Edson Arantes do Nascimento, but he was better known simply as Pelé. But Pelé, who played for Brazil, had retired. The New York Cosmos decided to offer him a huge contract to come out of retirement, and he agreed.

From that moment the popularity of soccer in the United States grew by leaps and bounds. Since Pelé was in the league, other stars of international fame joined various teams. Franz Beckenbauer of Germany and Giorgio Chinaglia of Italy signed with the Cosmos. George Best, a British player, came to the Los Angeles Aztecs, and Rodney March, also an Englishman, joined the Tampa Bay Rowdies. Other great players

The great Pelé greeting the crowds before his first game in the United States.

A soccer game always continues despite the rain. Here, Chinaglia plays during a downpour.

joined other clubs. In 1977, approximately three and a half million fans attended NASL games (more than ever before), and the championship game between the Cosmos and the Seattle Sounders attracted 35,548 cheering spectators.

It is obvious that American soccer can become a major team sport if it is given proper exposure and has star players. Even in other countries, soccer had humble beginnings. When the first English Cup match was held in south London, England on March 16, 1872, only 2000 people attended. But with the growth of the professional leagues, by 1901 the final match was watched by 110,000 fans, and TV and radio were still in the future. In 1923, in the new Wembley Stadium, the championship game almost caused a riot. Official figures put the attendance at 126,047, but the crowd was really almost 200,000! Today countless millions of fans attend matches in England, France, Brazil, China, Hungary, and other countries. Many more millions watch games on television or follow the play-by-play over the radio. Soccer is the world's most popular spectator sport.

And now crowds have begun filling the stands in the United States. The magnificent Pelé retired from soccer in 1977, and he played his last game for *both* teams—one half for the Cosmos, the other half for Santos of Brazil, the only other professional team he had played with. More than 77,000 adoring fans jammed the stadium to say farewell to their idol, even though it was really nothing more than an exhibition game.

Many soccer experts say that European soccer is better than American soccer, because it has more outstanding players. Perhaps this is true, but only temporarily. America can—and will—produce its own great players. And some day, maybe sooner than the experts think, an American team will win the World Cup, soccer's greatest prize.

3
SOCCER STARS: PAST, PRESENT, FUTURE

MOST BASEBALL FANS ARE FAMILIAR with the careers of such stars as Babe Ruth, Ted Williams, and Reggie Jackson. True football fans know about Red Grange, Jimmy Brown, and O. J. Simpson. In each example, one of the players was active about 50 years ago, another about 15 years ago, and the third is still a star player today.

The modern American soccer fan is probably unfamiliar with the stars of the past in the sport, perhaps because almost all of them played in other countries. Yet today's baseball owes a great debt to players like Ruth and Williams, because the game would not be the same if they had not played, and the same can be said of soccer. It would be almost impossible to list all of the soccer superstars of long ago, but merely to mention a few is to pay tribute to all of them.

Back in the 1870's, a swift young man named R. W. S. Vidal played for Oxford, England, and also for a team called the Wanderers. Vidal

A game among five-year-olds at Hicksville . . . the future Pelés.

earned the title "Prince of Dribblers" because of the way he could outmaneuver his opponents. In one match he scored three goals from kickoff in succession, dribbling all the way without ever losing possession of the ball. Another magnificent dribbler was A. F. Kinnaird, who also played for the Wanderers. In the 1873 Cup finals he dribbled almost the entire length of the field and scored against Oxford. It would be almost impossible in modern soccer for a player to dribble over the whole field and score, keeping possession all the time.

Some of the great soccer players have had amazingly long careers. For example, Billy Meredith, who helped found the Soccer Association (which is similar to America's Player Associations) was for 25 years, from 1895 to 1920, one of the sport's greatest outside right forwards. Another marvelous older player was Stanley Matthews, nicknamed "The Old Fox." In 1953, at the age of 38, Matthews inspired his Blackpool team to a come-from-behind victory over Bolton in the Cup finals. And Matthews continued to play a good game of soccer until he was 50 years old!

Bobby Charlton was probably the most popular of all English soccer players. In 1958 he was in a plane crash in Munich in which all his teammates were killed. Only Charlton survived. Eight years later he was back to reap glory for England as the captain of the team that won the coveted Jules Rimet Trophy, the World Series and Superbowl of soccer.

It is fortunate for the United States that some of the finest European players are now racing over American soccer fields. One of the best is Franz Beckenbauer of Germany, also called "The Kaiser." As well as being a great star, Beckenbauer has helped change the way soccer is played.

The great Bobby Orr helped change ice hockey in the same way Beckenbauer has changed his game. When Orr broke into hockey, defensemen seldom scored goals. But Orr was always in the thick of scoring plays. It was not unusual for him to score 29 or more goals and rack up 70 or more assists during a season.

Beckenbauer, now with the Cosmos, did the same thing while playing as captain of the Bayern Munich team, which won the Jules Rimet Trophy in 1974. His position was back—a defenseman—but he revolutionized the position by mounting strong attacks. For three straight years—1974, 1975, and 1976—he led his team to the European Cup championships. Twice, in 1972 and 1976, he was named European Footballer of the Year; in 1974 and 1975 he was the runner-up. In 1977 he played in only 15 games with the Cosmos, yet he scored 4 goals and had 5 assists.

Gordon Banks of the Fort Lauderdale Strikers is considered by many soccer experts to be

Beckenbauer ready to score.

the finest goalkeeper in the game, greater even than Russia's Lev Yashin. He too was in a terrible accident and made a remarkable comeback; in 1973 he suffered severe eye injuries in an auto crash, which put him on the sidelines for four years. In 1977 he returned to action with the Strikers, and was one of only two goalkeepers in the NASL to play every minute of every game on the regular schedule. In his comeback year he finished second to Ken Cooper of Dallas on the list of NASL Leading Goalkeepers. Banks racked up nine shutouts, and permitted an average of only 1.12 goals per game to be scored against his team.

One of the most colorful soccer players is George Best, who plays midfield for the Los Angeles Aztecs. Best is handsome, athletic, and was once considered the glamour boy of English soccer. But on the field he is all business. In the 1967–1968 season he was the leading scorer of the English First Division, with 28 goals, and he was named European Footballer of the Year in 1968. He and teammate Steve David set an NASL record by scoring a point each for ten straight games.

However, the greatest single player in the history of soccer, the undisputed king of the sport, was Edson Arantes do Nascimento, better known as King Pelé. He was the master dribbler, an accurate passer, and a selfless team player. When he kicked for the net the ball seemed to zoom as if it had been shot out of a cannon. He could dodge, he could feint, he could tackle, he could set up plays. He is a legend.

Pelé was born into a very poor family on October 23, 1940. His father was a fair soccer player, and the boy soon grew to love the game. How he got the nickname Pelé is not quite clear. Perhaps it was because he did not own a soccer ball when he was young, and used to kick almost anything that lay near his feet. The Portuguese word *pelada* means "a pickup game without proper equipment." Probably one of his friends simply shortened the word to Pelé. Many soccer players in Brazil had nicknames. Pelé's father was known as Dondinho.

Pelé was only 15 years old when he was given a tryout with the Santos team. Coach Luis Perez and the other players were impressed by the way the youngster moved the ball, and Pelé was given a contract to play with the Santos junior team. Three months later he was a member of the regular club.

For a time Pelé was a bench warmer, but he watched each game closely, learning something new every day. The following year he was a first-stringer.

Pelé was only 17 years old when the Brazilian team entered the World Cup matches for the prized Jules Rimet Trophy, in 1958. And it was Pelé who was the star. In the quarterfinals, against Wales, Pelé scored the only goal of the game. In the semifinals, against France, he scored three goals. Fans marveled at the little bundle of dynamite roaring down on the field. He was only five feet, six and a half inches tall and weighed a mere 145 pounds, but he was playing rings around opponents who were six inches taller and 50 pounds heavier.

In the finals, against Sweden, Pelé made one play that left the huge crowd gasping. Brazil was clinging to a narrow 2–1 lead and had to score another goal quickly to put the game on ice.

Surrounded by Swedish defensemen, Pelé saw the ball arcing toward him. With superb timing he leaped high above his opponents, stopping the ball with his right thigh, then bounced it over to his left thigh and up to his head. Still in the air, with his back to the goal, he bounced the ball still higher, then spun around and headed the ball into the net like a rocket. The goalkeeper hardly saw the ball. Brazil won the game and the championship.

Year after year, in spite of injuries and illness, Pelé continued to be soccer's greatest star. In 1959 he led Santos to the championship, scoring 125 goals, 45 of them in interleague competition. He was in the Brazilian army at the time, so of course he had to play for his military unit, and in these games he scored 14 more goals. He also played for the Brazilian national team, and scored an additional 11 goals.

Other teams all over the world tried to get Pelé from Santos, but Authie Coury, president

of the club, turned a deaf ear: "Pelé is not for sale at any price," he said. "Besides, if I did sell him, I think the Santos fans would kill me."

Opponents of Santos, realizing that the only way to beat the team was by stopping Pelé, often fouled the star viciously. Pelé was puzzled and angered, because he was a clean player and everyone knew it. Once Pelé became so angry over a foul that he tried to knock the offending player to the ground. The referee claimed he did not see the foul and Pelé was thrown out of the game. But the crowd had seen the foul and began to boo. Later, Pelé demanded a hearing to tell his side of the story. An investigation turned up the facts, and Pelé was cleared and the referee was suspended for 30 days.

On November 19, 1969, Pelé reached another milestone in his career. Playing in Rio de Janeiro before 90,000 fans, with 12 minutes left to play, Pelé banged one into the net. It was the 1000th goal of his remarkable career.

To describe Pelé's international fame is almost impossible. Once, his presence stopped a bloody war. During the conflict between Biafra and Nigeria, the Santos team was scheduled to play one game in each country. For that reason a two-day truce was declared. After the game in Nigeria, the Santos team crossed a river, which divided the two countries. Halfway across the Nigerian boat was met by a Biafran boat. The two enemy captains saluted each other, and the Nigerian captain said, "This is Pelé. Take the very best care of him."

Pelé retired from the Santos team, but in 1975 he came out of retirement and signed a three-year contract with the Cosmos, calling for a total payment of four and a half million dollars. He was 34 years old, and although still a great player, some of the magic of his earlier career was gone. Still, he made up in experience what he lacked in speed. He could still do things with a soccer ball that left opposing players staring in wonder.

At the end of the 1977 season Pelé announced his permanent retirement from active play. But he will always be remembered as the finest all-around soccer player ever to step onto a field.

So far the United States has had to get most of its star players from other lands. But in a few years that will change, because now millions of young Americans are playing the game in organized leagues throughout the nation.

"Youth Soccer" is open to boys and girls of all ages under 19. There are thousands of leagues in all sections of the country. In one New Jersey township there are about 2000 teams, each composed of at least 11 youngsters. Players are divided according to age groups, so that no team is overmatched against an older squad.

Girls are playing soccer in ever increasing numbers. In the Washington, D.C. area, there is a girls' soccer league composed of between

Running relays at a soccer clinic conducted by the
New York Apollos at a Hadassah day camp in
Queens, New York.

20,000 and 30,000 players. Some of the girls start playing the game at the age of six.

Most soccer officials say that by 1985 there will be five million—or more—young people playing amateur soccer in leagues and in schools.

And that is where the American stars of the future will come from!

Hicksville players and referee running in practice.

4

UNDERSTANDING SOCCER

SOCCER IS A COMPARATIVELY SIMPLE game to learn. There are surprisingly few rules, and they can be quickly mastered. It is only necessary to remember that not much body contact is permitted, although players can collide when they are going after the ball. Most of the rules, especially those involving fouls and misconduct, are a matter of common sense.

★ THE FIELD

A soccer field can vary in size. It must be between 100 and 130 yards long, and from 50 to 100 yards wide. The length of the field is divided by a *halfway line*, with a 30-foot circle in the middle of that line.

The goals are at the opposite ends of the field, in the middle of each *goal line*. The *goals* are 8 yards wide and 8 feet high, with a net attached to the side bars and the crossbar.

In front of the goal is the *goal area*. It extends 6 yards into the playing field and is 20 yards wide.

Surrounding the goal area is the *penalty area*. It is 44 yards wide and 18 yards long. There is a *penalty spot* in the middle of the penalty area, exactly 12 yards from the middle of the goal. In the middle of the penalty area, on its inside edge, is a semicircle, which has a 10-yard radius.

At each of the four corners of the field are the *corner areas*, quarter-circles marked by small flags. Each corner area has a radius of 1 yard.

★ THE BALL

A soccer ball is usually made of leather, but can also be made of any plastic material that is not harmful to the players. It weighs from 14 to 16 ounces and measures 27 to 28 inches in circumference.

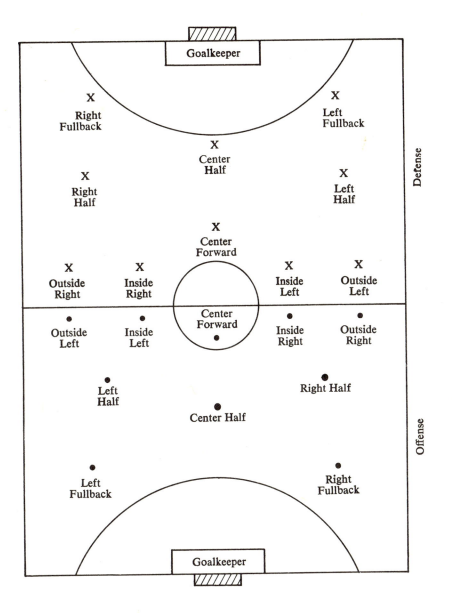

Game action at the goal.

★ DURATION OF THE GAME

A regulation soccer game consists of two 45-minute halves. Junior matches can consist of two 30-minute halves.

★ SOME SOCCER RULES

Beginning soccer players are sometimes confused by the terms Goal Kick, Corner Kick, Direct Free Kick, Indirect Free Kick, and Penalty Kick. Of course, each type of kick is different, and they are really not difficult to understand.

Rules for Goal Kicks and Corner Kicks

A Goal Kick and a Corner Kick are awarded when the ball has gone over the goal line and no goal was scored; possession is awarded to the opponents of the team which sent the ball over the goal line.

Goal Kick

If the player who last played the ball before it went over the goal line was on the attacking team, a Goal Kick is awarded to the defending team.

A Goal Kick is executed by the goalkeeper. The ball is spotted down in that part of the goal area closest to the place where it went across the goal line. He then kicks the ball out of the penalty area. The goalkeeper cannot touch the ball with his hands before he kicks it. He cannot play the ball again until another player has played it. The goalkeeper cannot score a goal on a Goal Kick—another player must play the ball before a goal can be scored. Obviously, for the goalie to score on his goal kick the ball would have to travel completely across the length of the field, and that is not likely to happen anyway. If the goalkeeper *does* play the ball before another player has a chance to, an Indirect Free Kick is awarded to the other team at the spot where the infringement took place.

Corner Kick

A Corner Kick is awarded to the attacking team if the player who last played the ball before it went over the goal line was on the defending team. The Corner Kick is executed from the corner area of the playing field nearest to the spot where the ball went over the goal line. A goal cannot be scored on a Corner Kick, because a player other than the one who took the Corner Kick must put the ball into the net. Nor can the kicker play the ball again until another player has touched the ball. If the kicker does try to play the ball again, an Indirect Free Kick is awarded the other team at the spot where the infraction took place. Also, no opposing player can be closer than 10 yards to the spot where the ball is kicked into play.

A kicking demonstration at a soccer camp for advanced players, both boys and girls, many of whom hope to become professionals.

Rules for Direct and Indirect Free Kicks

Direct Free Kicks and Indirect Free Kicks are awarded when a rule has been broken.

The officials can award a team a *Direct Free Kick* if their opponents break any of the following rules:

Fouls and Misconduct

(1) Kicking or trying to kick an opponent.

(2) Tripping or trying to trip an opponent by use of the legs, or stooping down in front or behind an opponent.

(3) Jumping at an opponent.

(4) Charging into an opponent in a violent manner.

(5) Charging into an opponent from behind, unless the opponent is obstructing.

(6) Striking an opponent.

(7) Pushing an opponent.

(8) Using the hands or arms to propel the ball.

In addition, if one of these rules is broken inside the penalty area, the referee can award the fouled team a Penalty Kick. (See: *Penalty Kick.*)

The official can award a team an *Indirect Free Kick* if their opponents break one of the following rules:

Fouls and Misconduct

(1) Playing in a manner considered dangerous by the referee. Example—trying to kick the ball while it is being held by the goalkeeper.

(2) Charging an opponent legally, but when neither player is within playing distance of the ball.

(3) Deliberately "obstructing"—getting between an opponent and the ball when neither player is within playing distance of the ball.

(4) Charging the goalkeeper, except when he is outside his own goal area, when he is holding the ball, or when the goalkeeper is obstructing.

(5) When the goalkeeper "carries the ball," meaning that he has the ball in his hands and has taken more than four steps without bouncing it on the ground.

(6) When a player is charged with "ungentlemanly conduct," or uses foul or abusive language against the referee.

A player can be cautioned for other minor infractions, such as entering the game without being permitted to do so by the referee's signal. In such situations no penalty is imposed.

A good save.

An attempted block.

Direct Free Kick

If a player attempting a *Direct* Free Kick can boot the ball into the net, it counts as a goal.

Indirect Free Kick

A player attempting an *Indirect* Free Kick cannot score a goal even if the ball does go into the net. The ball must be played by a teammate after it has traveled at least the distance of its own circumference.

Both Direct and Indirect Free Kicks are taken at the spot where the infraction occurred.

When a player attempts either a Direct or Indirect Free Kick from inside his own penalty area, all opponents must be outside that penalty area, and at least 10 yards away from the ball. The ball is not considered in play until it clears the penalty area. If the goalkeeper is attempting the kick, he cannot touch the ball with his hands. He must kick it into play from the spot where it is resting, otherwise the kick is taken over.

When a player attempts either a Direct or Indirect Free Kick from outside his own penalty area, all opposing players must be at least 10 yards away from the ball, unless they are standing on their own goal line between the goal posts. The ball is considered in play when it has traveled at least the distance of its own circumference.

Penalty Kick

If the defending team commits a foul in its own penalty area, and that foul would ordinarily call for a direct free kick, then the referee can award the attacking team a penalty kick.

The Penalty Kick is a one-on-one situation. The kick is taken from the penalty spot, which is inside the penalty area. Except for the goalkeeper and the player who will be kicking the ball, all players on both teams must be outside the penalty area. The goalkeeper must stand still on his own goal line, between the goal posts, until the ball is kicked. The kicker must kick the ball forward at least the distance of its own circumference. At that point the ball is in play. The kicker cannot play the ball again until another player touches it or plays it, or else an Indirect Free Kick will follow.

As with an ordinary Direct Free Kick, the kicker will be credited with a goal if he can put the ball into the net.

If a defensive player causes an infringement on a Penalty Kick and a goal is *not* scored, the kick will be taken over.

If an attacking player causes an infringement on a Penalty Kick and a goal is scored, the goal will not count. The kick will be taken over.

Offside rules do not apply during a Penalty Kick.

Offside

The team that is in possession of the ball is the only side that can be offside. As a general rule, a player or team can be offside in two ways:

(1) If he is nearer his opponent's goal than the ball at the moment when the ball is played.

(2) If there are fewer than two defensive players between the man playing the ball and the goal.

However, there are certain *exceptions* to the offside rule. A player is *not* offside if:

(1) He is in his own half of the field.

(2) There are two opponents nearer to their own goal line than he is.

(3) The ball was last touched or played by an opponent.

(4) He receives the ball direct from a Goal Kick, a Corner Kick, a Throw-in; or when the ball was dropped by the referee.

In 1973, the North American Soccer League introduced a variation of the offside rule. Traditionally, the midfield stripe is the dividing line in determining an offside (see: exception 1). By NASL rules, there is another line, called the "Blue Line," running the width of the field 35 yards from each goal line. Under this rule an attacking player is not offside until he crosses this Blue Line. However, it is *only* in the NASL that the Blue Line exists. Under Olympic rules, the midfield line is still the dividing line.

In determining an offside, everything depends on where the ball is in relation to where the offensive player is. And when a player is offside, he cannot interfere with an opponent. He cannot station himself so close to the goalkeeper or any other opponent as to hamper the opponent's movement. He cannot obstruct an opponent. If the offending player is guilty of breaking such rules, the referee can penalize him.

The penalty for an offside is an Indirect Free Kick taken by an opponent at the point where the violation occurred.

Ball out of Bounds

When the ball goes out of bounds over the side lines (called *touch lines* in soccer), it is awarded to the opposing team of the last player who touched or played the ball before it went out of bounds. This is *not* the same as the ball going over the goal line, when a Goal Kick or Corner Kick is awarded.

In these cases, the ball is thrown in from the spot where it crossed the touch line. The player throwing the ball into play cannot touch the ball again until it has been played by another player. A goal cannot be scored by means of a throw-in.

Scoring

A goal is scored when the ball passes over the goal line between the goal posts and under the crossbar. A goal *cannot* be scored by throwing the ball, or by carrying the ball, or by forcing the ball into the net by the use of hands or arms.

5

FUNDAMENTALS OF PLAYING SOCCER

★ THE PLAYERS

A soccer team consists of 11 players. Usually, the positions are filled as follows:

Five *forwards*, three *halfbacks*, two *fullbacks*, and the *goalkeeper*.

Sometimes, especially among the pros, the positions are called by other names. For example, the halfbacks can be called "Midfielders" or "linkmen" and the fullbacks may be called "defenders." But in many ways the old names are better, because they make it easier for a young player to understand each position's responsibilities.

The forwards are the front line of attack. Usually they are the best passers, dribblers, and kickers on the team. They score almost all the goals.

The halfbacks are generally the best all-round players on the team. They have to be able to help out on offense, but they are also considered the first line of defense. They try to stop their opponents' attack before it penetrates too deeply into their half of the field.

The fullbacks are primarily defensive players. Often, if an opponent can get by the fullbacks, there is no one left to stop a goal except the goalkeeper. The fullbacks must know how to work closely with the goalkeeper.

The goalkeeper is the last line of defense. He guards the net. He must have lightning reflexes to stop hard kicks at point blank range. Often he will have to leap high in order to deflect a kick up over the crossbar, or dive to the side to make a save, or smother the ball with his body. The goalkeeper is the only player on a soccer team permitted to use his hands.

A beautifully executed goalie save. The goalkeeper is the only player allowed to catch the ball with his hands.

★ CONDITIONING

A young athlete must be in better condition to play soccer than any other team sport.

Baseball players do not have to run very far or for long periods of time. They can rest between half-innings. Football players go into a huddle after every play, which gives them time for a breather. Hockey players move fast, but they are on the ice for only a few minutes at a time. Basketball players do run a lot, but often the action stops while someone shoots a couple of fouls. Also, substitutions are frequent in basketball. There are far fewer substitutions in soccer.

Soccer players need good legs and stamina. They are constantly running, jumping, and kicking. Soccer players also need strong neck muscles in order to head the ball (see *Heading the Ball*).

Building Speed and Stamina

The best exercise is a combination of jogging and wind sprints. The jogging helps build stamina, or long-distance staying power, while the sprints increase the runner's speed.

If you are just starting to get in condition, do so slowly. The first time out start with a jog of about half a mile, then do some walking, go back to jogging, and finish with a fast sprint. As the days and weeks go by, the distance should be increased. In about two months you should be jogging about three miles, with wind sprints

Pelé is in top shape, ready to spring into action at any moment. Here, he's at a pre-game warm-up.

every quarter of a mile and *no walking at all*. All sprints should be at least 50 yards.

It is best to wear running shoes, not sneakers. Good sweat socks help prevent foot blisters.

Building Strong, Limber Muscles

Calisthenics are ideal as body-building and muscle-loosening exercises. When you first start, do each exercise only five or six times. Progress slowly, adding one every day or every other day, until you work up to the recommended number.

All the exercises given should be performed every day. It does no good to skip a couple of days, because the muscles will lose their tone.

(1) Side-Straddle Hop (Jumping Jacks): Start with the feet together, hands on hips. At the count of one, hop so that both feet are out to the sides and the hands clap together overhead. At the count of two return to the starting position. Repeat the exercise at least 20 times.

(2) Knee-Bend Rock: Start with the feet together, hands on hips. At the count of one, bend the trunk so that the tips of the fingers touch the toes, keeping the knees straight. At the count of two, squat down so that the body's weight is on the toes, and the backs of the thighs rest against the heels. At the count of three return to the second position. At the count of four return to starting position. This

Limbering up before a game.

Hicksville players warming up.

exercise should be performed crisply, at least 20 times.

(3) Situps. Lie flat on your back, arms at your sides. At the count of one sit up and bend the body forward, touching fingertips to your toes. At the count of two return to starting position.

(Some readers, when first attempting situps, might find them difficult. A friend can help by holding down the exerciser's feet, at least in the beginning.)

The situp exercise can be varied. The exercise can be begun with the hands laced behind the head. When sitting up, the body twists, so that the right elbow is pointed at the left knee. Then the left elbow is pointed at the right knee.

Situps help build strong abdominal muscles. Repeat at least 20 times.

(4) Pushups. Begin with the body supported by the arms, hands flat on the floor, about a shoulder width apart. The legs are held straight back, with only the toes touching the floor. At the count of one, lower the body so that the chest *almost* touches the floor. The legs and back must remain straight. At the count of two, raise the body to starting position. This exercise strengthens the arms and upper back muscles. Repeat 20 times.

(5) Neck Rotation. Heading the ball is an important move in soccer. Strong neck muscles are needed.

Stand with feet slightly spread, hands on hips. Rotate the head a dozen times to the left, then a dozen times to the right.

(6) Stomach Rocker. Lie flat on the floor, face down, hands clasped behind your back. Force the head and torso up, then rock forward and raise up the legs. This should set up a "rocking motion" with the weight resting on the stomach. Repeat at least 20 times.

Personal Habits

Good physical condition depends a great deal on proper personal habits. For example:

Don't smoke. Smoking is poison. It cuts down on stamina, blackens the lungs, and can even lead to serious illness.

Get plenty of sleep. During sleep the body

repairs itself and stores up energy for another day. Growing youngsters need 9 hours of sleep every night.

Avoid alcoholic drinks. Beer is fattening and puts a "rubber tire" around the middle of the body. Hard liquor contains a lot of "empty calories," which can also lead to a paunchy middle.

Watch your diet. Rich cakes and pies are permitted once in a while, but not too often. Broiled foods are better than fried foods because they contain less fat for the body to digest. A proper diet should include lean meats, chicken, fish, eggs, whole grains in bread and cereals, cheeses, vegetables, and milk. Coffee and tea should be avoided. Cold soda pop tastes good, but a young athlete should go easy on such drinks. Substitute fruit juice or cool water.

★ PLAYING THE GAME

Soccer is mostly a kicking game.

There are several different ways to kick the ball, but it must be remembered that nearly always—except for a kick on goal—a kick is really a pass from a player to a teammate. A long kick that zooms upfield and lands where there is no teammate to receive it is useless. Accuracy is more important than distance. The best kick is a controlled kick.

A kick using the toe of the foot can travel like a

A satisfying kick.

45★

An instep kick being executed in practice.

bullet, but that type should be used only for a close-in shot on goal. Otherwise, it just is not accurate enough. The instep of the foot affords better kicking control than the toe, although the instep kick will not travel as far or as fast as a toe kick. The side of the foot is even better for control than the instep, but the kick will travel even a shorter distance. Kick passes can also be executed with the sole and the heel of the foot.

The Instep Kick

Executing the Instep Kick properly depends on whether the ball is stationary, rolling toward the kicker, or rolling away from the kicker. Each situation requires different timing.

If the ball is rolling away, the player must first catch up with it; this may take two or three strides. If the ball is rolling toward the player, only one short stride may be needed. A stationary ball is the least troublesome of all.

To be in proper position, the nonkicking foot is planted a couple of inches to the sides of the ball, with the arch of the foot even with the center of the ball. The kicking leg swings forward, knee slightly bent, toe pointed down and in. The foot makes contact with the ball at the lower part of the shoelaces.

The Instep Kick—Photos above show the correct position of the kicking foot (the right foot); photos below show the correct position of the non-kicking foot (the left).

Inside Of Foot Kick

For passing and for ball control in short distance situations, the ball can be kicked with the inside part of the foot.

As with the Instep Kick, this method also requires proper timing, depending on whether the ball is rolling or stationary.

The foot makes contact with the ball just below the ankle, between the big toe and the heel. This provides a good, flat kicking area. The kicking foot should be about an inch or so above the ground.

The Inside of Foot Kick—Note that in photo at far right, the foot makes contact with the ball just below the ankle, between the toe and heel.

Outside Of Foot Kick

This type of kick–pass is accurate, and can be used to fool an opponent. The kicker can feint an Inside of Foot Kick, tap the ball to the outside, and go around the player guarding him. The foot makes contact with the ball just below the ankle, between the heel and little toe.

Heel Kick

The Heel Kick is useful as a backward pass to a teammate coming up from behind. But it is tricky and can be dangerous. If not timed exactly right, the kicker might accidentally step on the ball and twist an ankle. It is best to use the Heel Kick when the ball is stationary.

The nonkicking leg should be ahead of the ball. The kicking foot comes up over the ball, and the heel taps it smartly backward.

Lift or Lob Kick

When an opponent is close to the kicker, and a teammate is behind the opponent in position to receive a pass, a Lob Kick will lift the ball over the defensive player's head.

Basically, a Lob Kick is something like a chip shot in golf. Height is more important than distance. Properly executed, the ball will rise up, travel a short distance and come down in the target area.

The nonkicking foot is behind and to the side of the ball. The kicking foot makes contact with the ball at the upper part of the shoe. The body should lean back slightly to help give the ball some lift.

Toe Kick

To Toe Kick is usually not very accurate, but the ball will travel faster than it would if kicked with the instep. Therefore, a Toe Kick should be used mostly as a shot on goal.

A Toe Kick is the same as the Instep Kick, except that the toe is used. The player's timing should still depend on whether the ball is rolling toward the kicker, away from the kicker, or is stationary.

The Toe Kick, powerfully executed.

Volley Kick

Often during a game a player will have to execute a kick while the ball is in the air. Perfect timing and body position are very important.

The ball should be dropping down as the Volley Kick is begun, and kicked when it is as close to the ground as possible without actually bouncing.

The body should be leaning back slightly. The kicking foot comes up, knee bent, toe pointed down and in, the ankle locked. All the player's weight is on the nonkicking leg. The ball is kicked with the inside part of the instep.

If the ball is still too high when the Volley Kick is attempted, it will pop almost straight up in the air without traveling very far upfield. Actually, if the body is leaning back enough, and the ball is high enough, it is possible for a player to kick the ball backward over his head.

The Volley Kick—In this practice session for the volley kick, the ball is kicked backward over the head.

Half-Volley Kick

In a way the Half-Volley is the opposite of a Volley Kick. In the Volley Kick the ball is coming down. In the Half-Volley, the ball has bounced and is starting to rise. Foot meets ball on the short hop.

The Half-Volley is really a basic Instep Kick, except that the ball is a couple of inches in the air when the foot makes contact. If the Half-Volley is executed properly, the ball will zoom away like a rising line drive.

The Half-Volley Kick—Note that the ball is a couple of inches in the air when the foot makes contact.

Pivot Kick

The Pivot Kick is one of the most effective of all long-distance kicks. It is used in corner kicks, and also to cross the ball far over to the opposite side of the field.

The kicker approaches the ball and plants his weight firmly on the nonkicking foot, about 18 inches behind and to the side of the ball. The body is leaning back slightly, and the hips pivot as the kick is executed. The kicking foot is pointed down and slightly in, and contact is made with the instep.

The Pivot Kick—Note how the hips pivot as the kick is executed.

With all types of kicks and passes there are certain fundamentals to remember:

(1) Try to keep your eye on the ball at all times.

(2) Remember to follow through on all kicks.

(3) Plant the nonkicking foot firmly before kicking, otherwise you are liable to slip.

(4) Try to judge the ball's target area. A kick that sails too far or falls short can result in loss of possession.

(5) Whenever possible, kicks should be short ones. Long kicks can be intercepted more easily.

(6) A good kicker can kick equally well with either foot. This takes a lot of practice.

(7) Never "telegraph" a kick. Try to keep your opponent guessing until the last second. Practice feinting a kick in one direction, but kicking in the opposite direction. Practice feinting a kick with one foot, then kicking with the other foot.

★ DRIBBLING

Dribbling in soccer is like dribbling in basketball, except that in soccer it is done with short, swift kicks instead of by bouncing the ball with the hands. A good dribbler can get around an opponent guarding him by moving to either side, or even by kicking the ball between his opponent's feet, dodging around, and then catching up with the ball again.

The average distance a dribble rolls is 16 to 18 inches, although it can be shorter when the dribbler is being closely guarded. If the dribbler is not closely guarded, the ball might travel 2 or 3 feet.

All types of kicks are involved in dribbling. Much of the time a quick Instep Kick is used, but the Inside of Foot Kick, Outside of Foot Kick, and Heel Kick are also effective. When the dribbler mixes his kicks, especially using both feet, he can be hard to stop.

There are two fundamentals important in dribbling, which will help the player maintain possession of the ball:

(1) Try to keep your body between the ball and the player guarding you.

(2) Sometimes you may be forced to take your eyes off the ball, to find out where your opponent is, or to find an open teammate who can receive a pass. Take a quick look around, see where everyone is, then focus attention on the ball again.

★ TACKLING

A tackle in soccer means trying to gain possession of the ball while it is being played by an opponent. Unlike American football, a soccer tackle has a minimum of contact. It is done with the feet; the target is the ball, not the player. Charging into the player in possession is a foul.

Most of the time a tackle is attempted from either the front or the side of the player in possession. It is perfectly legal to tackle from behind, except that it is very tricky. The would-be tackler runs the risk of tripping his opponent, and that is also a foul.

The best way to execute a tackle is to get your opponent off balance while he is dribbling. It is legal to use your shoulder (but *not* to shove your opponent roughly aside) and make him go off stride. Using the inside or outside of the foot the tackler can sometimes tap the ball away from the player in possession.

Capitalizing on a mistake can result in a tackle. Your opponent may have dribbled a little too far to catch up with the ball. A quick burst of speed and you can beat him to it, or boot the ball through your opponent's legs.

It is also possible, when running shoulder-to-shoulder with an opponent in possession, to move ahead of him slightly, then tap the ball backward with the heel of the foot.

A well-executed tackle.

A sliding tackle is spectacular, but the tackler must be careful not to trip his opponent. To execute a sliding tackle, the tackler judges the speed and direction of his opponent, then slides feet first toward the path of the ball, kicking it away.

All these fundamentals must be practiced again and again. Soccer is an outstanding sport, easy to learn but difficult to play well. Only those in the best physical condition, with speed of foot and a clear eye, can succeed.

Bouncing the ball off the knee in game action.

6
GLOSSARY OF SOCCER TERMS

ATTACKER One of the forwards of a soccer team. The attackers do most of the scoring.

BACKUP A player trailing behind a teammate to help out if necessary.

BEHIND When an attacker kicks the ball past the goal line, the ball is said to be "behind." If it is kicked there by a defender, the attacking team is awarded a corner kick.

BYE When the ball passes the goal line and goes behind, it is called a "bye."

CARRYING When the goalkeeper carries the ball more than four steps without bouncing it, he is guilty of "carrying."

CENTER THE BALL A pass from near the sidelines to the center of the field.

CHARGING Running into an opponent violently. This is a foul, and the referee can award the opposing team a Direct Free Kick.

CLEARING KICK Kicking the ball away from one's own goal.

CORNER AREA A small arc with a radius of 1 yard in each of the four corners of the field.

CORNER KICK An Indirect Free Kick taken by an attacker from one of the corner areas.

CROSSING KICK A ball kicked from one side of the field to the other.

DECOY PLAY A play designed to draw an opponent away from an area so that there is an opening in the defense.

DEFENSIVE END OF FIELD The half of the field defended by a team.

DIRECT FREE KICK A free kick awarded because of a personal foul. A goal can be scored on a Direct Free Kick.

DRIBBLE Short kicks taken with the instep or side of the foot to advance the ball.

FIRST TIME KICK Kicking the ball without first trapping it, such as Volley Kick.

GOAL AREA The area in front of a goal, 20 yards wide and 6 yards deep.

GOAL KICK   An Indirect Free Kick. If an attacker kicks the ball over the end goal line, the goalkeeper kicks the ball from the front corner of the goal area on the side nearest to where it left the playing field.

GOAL LINES   The lines at the ends of the playing field.

HALFWAY LINE   The line which divides the length of the field in half. A 30-foot circle cuts through its middle.

HANDLING   Touching the ball with the hands. Only the goalkeeper is permitted to handle the ball.

HEADING   Making contact with the ball with the forehead.

INDIRECT FREE KICK   An award for a technical foul. A goal cannot be scored on an Indirect Free Kick.

KICKING TO A SPOT   Kicking the ball to an open area where a moving teammate can reach it.

KICKOFF   At the beginning of each period, or following a goal, the ball is put in play again by means of a kick from the center of the field into the opposing team's half of the field.

LEADING PASS   Same as *Kicking to a Spot.*

LOB   A high, soft kick which sails over a defensive player's head.

MARKING   Guarding a player.

OBSTRUCTING   Blocking out an opposing player without making contact with him.

PENALTY AREA   The area around a goal. It is 44 yards wide and 18 yards long. A goalkeeper cannot use his hands outside this area.

PENALTY KICK   A Direct Free Kick from 12 yards in front of the goal. If a player commits a personal foul in the Penalty Area, the opposing team is awarded a Penalty Kick.

PENALTY SPOT   The spot from which a Penalty Kick is taken.

PITCH   The field of play is called a pitch in soccer.

SAVE   Stopping a shot at the goal.

SWEEPER   A defensive player who roams either in front of or behind the defensive line to pick up stray passes.

SWITCH   When one player takes over the area usually covered by a teammate, and the teammate in turn covers the first player's area.

TACKLE   When a defensive player steals the ball away from an opponent.

THROW-IN   When the ball goes across the side lines, it is awarded to an opponent of the last player to touch or play the ball, who throws the ball into play. The throw-in must be made using both hands.

TOUCH LINES   The side lines (*not* the goal lines).

TRAPPING   Stopping the flight of the ball with the legs or body to gain control of the play.

VOLLEY   To kick the ball on the fly, before it touches the ground.

WALL PASS   A kind of "give-and-go" play. A player passes to a teammate and takes a return pass.

INDEX